JUSTIN BIEBER
ANNUAL 2012

MILLIE ROWLANDS

PROFILE

Full name: Justin Drew Bieber

Born: March 1, 1994

Star sign: Pisces

Height: 5' 3½'

Siblings: Half-sister named Jazmine and a half-brother named Jackson

Pet: Dog named Sam

Nicknames: Bieber, J-Beebs, Bieb

Hometown: Stratford, Ontario, Canada

Current home: Atlanta, Georgia

Car: A Range Rover bought for him by Usher for his 'Super Sweet 16'. Suweet!

Label: Island Def Jam

Hero: Chuck Norris

BIEBER FEVER

It would cost $2000 to $8000 per hour to have Justin Bieber singing at your birthday party!

Favourite slang term: 'Shawty'

Favourite sports: Ice hockey, soccer, and baseball

Girlfriends: None

Celebrity crush: Beyoncé

Favourite colour: Blue

Favourite food: Spaghetti and tacos

Favourite cereal: Captain Crunch

Favourite number: Six

Dislikes: Bling

Drinks: Vitamin water

Foreign languages: French and he can count to ten in German!

Phobias: Escalators and lifts as he suffers from claustrophobia

Favourite pie: Apple pie

Favourite candy: Sour patch kids

Favourite colour to wear: Purple

Favourite sports team: Toronto Maple Leafs

Favourite animal: Giraffe

Best friends: Ryan Butler, Christian Beadles and Chaz Somers

YouTube account: Kidrauhl

Favourite show: Smallville

Favourite movie: Rocky

Favourite saying: 'Single and Ready to Mingle'

Favourite subjects: Maths and English

Dislikes: Chocolate (except Twix!)

Party trick: He can solve a rubik's cube in under a minute

Favourite shoe brand: Supra

Favourite romantic movie: *A Walk To Remember*. Awww!

Favourite artists: Usher, Ne-Yo, Chris Brown, some 2Pac, Rascall Flatts, Elliott Yamin, Billy Talent, Lifehouse, and T-bone

INTRODUCING JUSTIN!

OMG! Bieber fever has well and truly taken over the world! To his army of dedicated fans, the Beliebers, he's the greatest popstar ever! The guy's got it all. He sings, raps and break-dances. He plays the guitar, piano, drums and the trumpet. Not to mention, he's super cute!

In less than a year, the Canadian kid with nothing more than pure talent and a laptop, rocket launched his career into the stratosphere. It wasn't long ago that the young star was just a regular child with a passion for music and a pipe dream. Now all his fantasies are more than a reality and he's the most famous and talented kid on the planet. You can't switch on a television or radio without a glimpse or mention of him. His crisp voice and cheeky face is imprinted on the hearts of fans everywhere. And, to think, his journey has only just begun...

TRUE BELIEBER

'On my wall I have a picture of James Dean, a poster of Entourage, The Hangover poster, a picture of 2Pac. I've also got a poster of a mouse with headphones on.'

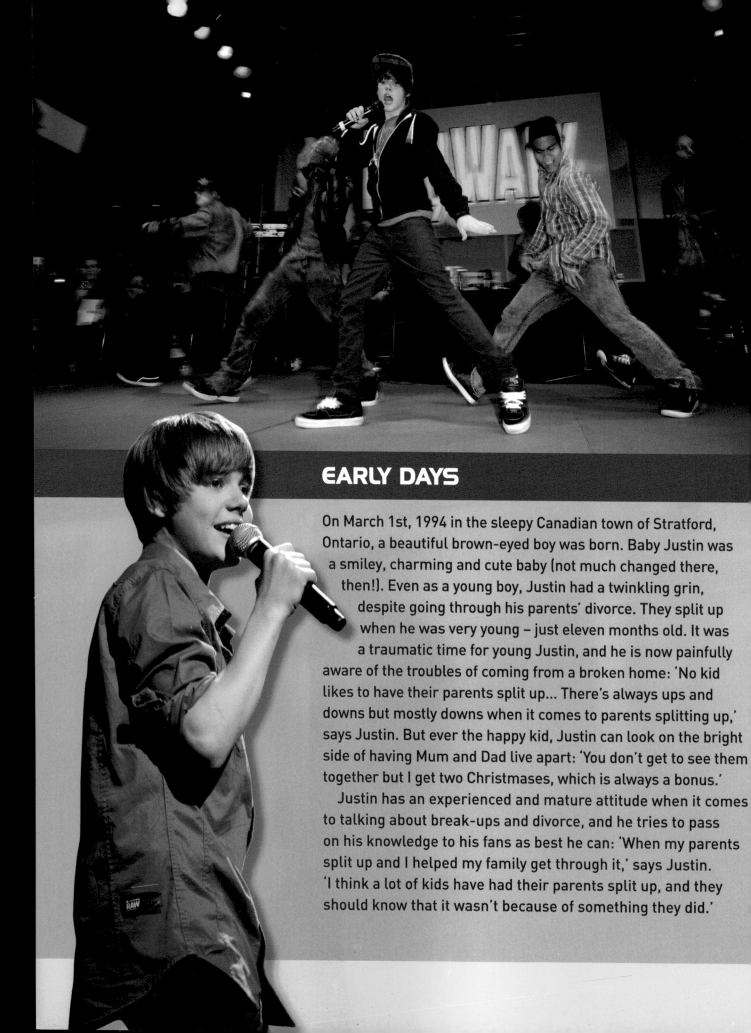

EARLY DAYS

On March 1st, 1994 in the sleepy Canadian town of Stratford, Ontario, a beautiful brown-eyed boy was born. Baby Justin was a smiley, charming and cute baby (not much changed there, then!). Even as a young boy, Justin had a twinkling grin, despite going through his parents' divorce. They split up when he was very young – just eleven months old. It was a traumatic time for young Justin, and he is now painfully aware of the troubles of coming from a broken home: 'No kid likes to have their parents split up... There's always ups and downs but mostly downs when it comes to parents splitting up,' says Justin. But ever the happy kid, Justin can look on the bright side of having Mum and Dad live apart: 'You don't get to see them together but I get two Christmases, which is always a bonus.'

Justin has an experienced and mature attitude when it comes to talking about break-ups and divorce, and he tries to pass on his knowledge to his fans as best he can: 'When my parents split up and I helped my family get through it,' says Justin. 'I think a lot of kids have had their parents split up, and they should know that it wasn't because of something they did.'

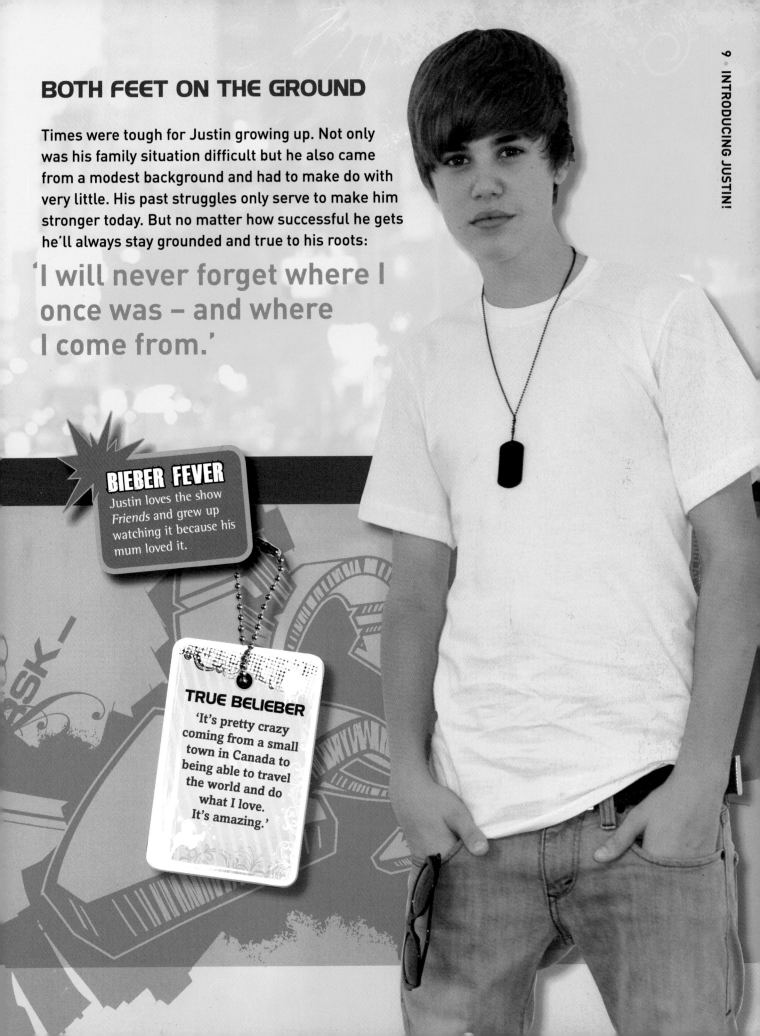

BOTH FEET ON THE GROUND

Times were tough for Justin growing up. Not only was his family situation difficult but he also came from a modest background and had to make do with very little. His past struggles only serve to make him stronger today. But no matter how successful he gets he'll always stay grounded and true to his roots:

'I will never forget where I once was – and where I come from.'

BIEBER FEVER

Justin loves the show *Friends* and grew up watching it because his mum loved it.

TRUE BELIEBER

'It's pretty crazy coming from a small town in Canada to being able to travel the world and do what I love. It's amazing.'

justin bieber quiz

Think you know everything there is to know about our superstar? Take the Bieber quiz and see how many points you score to see if you're Justin's biggest Belieber!

Test your friends and see who knows Justin the best.

1. What is Justin's middle name?
A) Mark
B) Andrew
C) Drew
D) He doesn't have one!

2. What year was Justin born?
A) 1990
B) 1995
C) 1993
D) 1994

3. What is Justin's star sign?
A) Aquarius
B) Leo
C) Taurus
D) Pisces

4. What is Justin's Youtube name?
A) Kidkanevil
B) Kidrauhl
C) Kidstar
D) Bieberfever

5. What is Justin's pet dog called?
A) Sammy
B) Spot
C) Sonny
D) Sylvester

6. Which of the following is NOT one of Justin's nicknames?
A) J-Beebs
B) Bieber
C) Beeb
D) J-Bone

7. What is Justin's favourite TV Show?
A) *Smallville*
B) *Jersey Shore*
C) *Cribs*
D) *Glee*

8. Who is Justin's all-time hero?
A) Usher
B) Michael Jackson
C) Chuck Norris
D) Bruce Lee

9. How old was Justin when he had his first kiss?
A) 16
B) 12
C) 14
D) 13

10. Who is the inspiration for Justin's look?
A) Zac Efron
B) Enrique Iglesias
C) Robbie Williams
D) James Dean

11. Which rap star appears on Justin's track, 'Baby'?
A) Ludacris
B) Ne-yo
C) Usher
D) Jay Z

12. Which nationality is Justin?
A) American
B) Australian
C) Canadian
D) British

13. Which popstar just missed out on signing Justin before he signed for Usher?

A) Jay Z

B) Eminem

C) Justin Timberlake

D) Kanye West

14. Which instrument does Justin NOT know how to play?

A) Trumpet

B) Saxophone

C) Drums

D) Guitar

15. When Justin first started making money from music what did he spend it on?

A) A holiday

B) A new car

C) A guitar

D) A laptop

16. What did Usher buy Justin for his 16th birthday?

A) A private jet

B) A speedboat

C) A house

D) A car

17. Where does Justin currently live?

A) Atlanta

B) New York

C) Los Angeles

D) Toronto

18. What are Justin's half-brother and half-sisters called?

A) Jessie and Jeremy

B) Josie and Johnny

C) Jennifer and Joseph

D) Jazmine and Jackson

19. What is Justin's favourite colour to wear?

A) Black

B) Purple

C) White

D) Red

20. Who is Justin's best friend in the world?

A) Usher

B) Leo DiCaprio

C) Ryan Butler

D) His mother

For answers see p61.

HOW MANY DID YOU SCORE? ADD UP YOUR POINTS TO SEE HOW MUCH OF A JUSTIN KNOW-IT-ALL YOU ARE.

15-20 – You know more about Justin than he knows about himself – you're his number one Belieber!

10-15 – Wow, you really know your stuff – you're a top Belieber.

5-10 – You know your Justin facts, but not enough – you're a could-do-better Belieber.

0-5 – You need to get studying up on your Justin knowledge – you're a half-hearted Belieber.

SCHOOL DAYS

While home life was tough for Justin in the early days, school wasn't much better. Justin and his mum didn't have much money and it was often difficult for them to afford the basic requirements for school, such as books and stationary.

BIEBER FEVER
Once Justin got an 'F' in school, but he changed it to a 'B', so he wouldn't get in trouble.

Justin never quite fitted into school life. He could never afford all the fancy clothes some of the other kids had and he got bullied for being small. But Justin reckons his early troubles have made him all the stronger: 'I didn't have as much as other people did,' says Justin. 'I think it made me stronger as a person – it built my character.'

BIEBER FEVER
Justin is the most searched for person on the Internet.

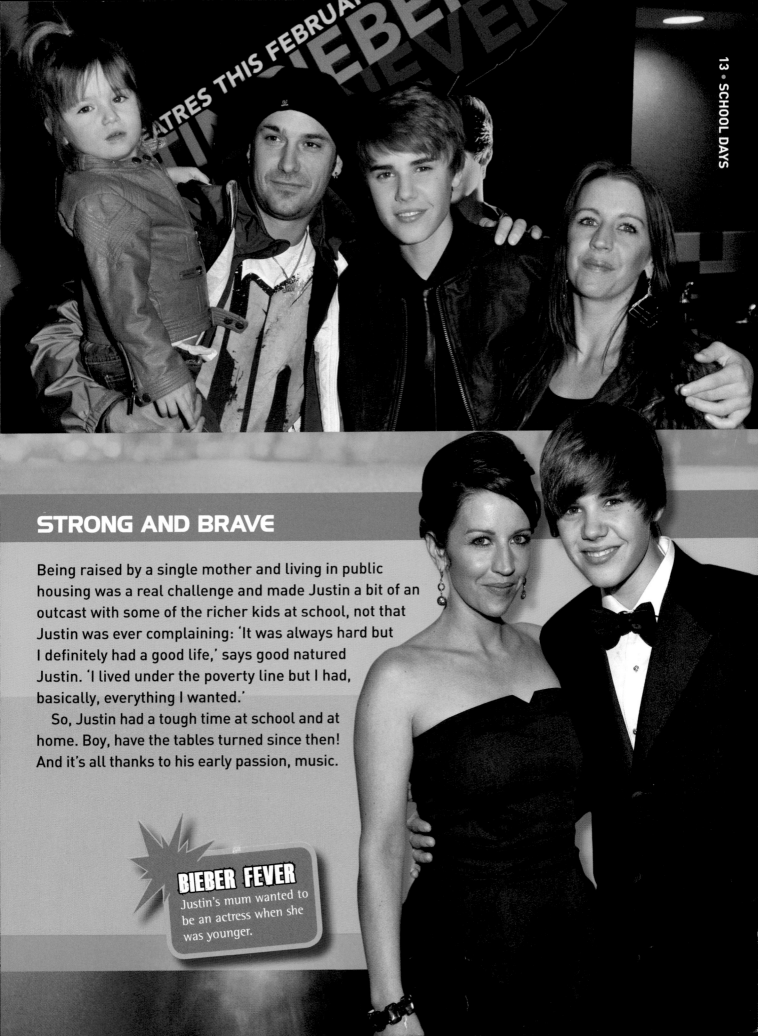

STRONG AND BRAVE

Being raised by a single mother and living in public housing was a real challenge and made Justin a bit of an outcast with some of the richer kids at school, not that Justin was ever complaining: 'It was always hard but I definitely had a good life,' says good natured Justin. 'I lived under the poverty line but I had, basically, everything I wanted.'

So, Justin had a tough time at school and at home. Boy, have the tables turned since then! And it's all thanks to his early passion, music.

BIEBER FEVER

Justin's mum wanted to be an actress when she was younger.

it's written in the stars

Make your very own fortuneteller to find out what yours and Justin Bieber's destiny holds.

Fill your Justin fortunes with great predictions such as...

You're Justin's true love!

Justin to be world's greatest star!

You're Justin's best pal!

Justin is so over you!

Instructions

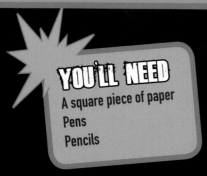

1. Find the middle of the paper by folding it from corner to corner.

2. Fold each corner to the centre to make a smaller square.

3. Turn the square over, and turn each corner to the centre again to make an even smaller square.

4. Turn over again. Draw a different colour on each quarter of the square.

5. Turn over again. Put numbers 1 – 8 on each segment

6. Open out each flap and write a message behind each number.

7. Put the thumb and forefinger of each hand into a segment and close up the fortune-teller. First ask your pal to chose a colour . If they choose BLUE, spell out B-L-U-E and open and shut the fortune-teller four times. Then ask your pal to choose a number from the four numbers showing. Open and shut the fortune-teller however many times they choose. Then finally ask them to choose another number, open up the flap and read them the message.

MUSIC

Justin's escape was his music. But it became pretty clear that it would be more than just a hobby to help him through difficult times. He was extremely gifted from the outset, picking instruments and getting the hang of them almost immediately. 'I started to play the drums at two years old, then I picked up the piano at eight, but I've never had a lesson.'

BIEBER FEVER
Justin's a lefty! What hand do you play the guitar with?

'Basically when I started playing the guitar, I picked up a right-handed guitar . . . It was difficult because it's backwards.'

BIEBER FEVER
The single 'One Time' isn't directed to a specific girl, it's directed at all girls.

GUITAR HERO

Initially Justin found it hard playing the guitar, as they were all the wrong way round! But he soon realised that he needed a left-handed instrument. 'At eight I started to play the guitar,' says Justin. 'Basically when I started playing the guitar, I picked up a right-handed guitar . . . It was difficult because it's backwards. My mum, I think it was for my birthday, she bought me a left-handed guitar. And so ever since I was young I learned on a left-handed guitar.'

It soon became clear that Justin could earn a few dollars from his talents, so he took to the streets, playing songs in the hope of making the odd buck. It turned out he made a bit more than that: 'I used to play my guitar in my local city, so I would play outside and open up my guitar case, which people would throw in any change. I made $3,000 dollars and took my mum on a vacation to Florida. That was pretty awesome.'

BIEBER FEVER
Justin says 'Never' 69 times in the song 'Never Say Never'.

SING STAR

Despite all these many musical instruments coming naturally to Justin, it was singing that the pop star has become world renowned for. Justin's singing skills first began to gain recognition when he entered a local song contest, Stratford Idol, near his hometown in Canada. Justin performed Aretha Franklin's 'Respect', Matchbox 20's '3am', Alicia Keys's 'Fallin' and Ne-Yo's 'So Sick'. Amazingly, even with that awesome playlist, Justin didn't win! Can you believe it? Justin was just pipped in the final and came second. But he's no sore loser and was happy just having people appreciate his music.

Justin got high praise from the judges who were impressed with his vocal range. Sadly many of his friends and family couldn't make the live performance of the competition. So Natalie, his mother, made a decision that would change Justin's life and posted her son's performance on YouTube. Justin Bieber was online and the world would never be the same again.

TRUE BELIEBER

The 'Baby' music video is now the most watched music video ever on YouTube.

BIEBER FEVER

Justin once admitted that he cried because of the 'haters' comments online.

2011 Brit Awards
International Breakthrough Artist

2011 JUNO Awards
Best Album

2011 Kids Choice Awards
Favorite Male Singer
Favorite Song ('Baby')

2010 BET Awards
Best New Artist

2010 American Music Awards
Artist of the Year
Favorite Pop/Rock Male Artist
T-Mobile Breakthrough Artist
Favorite Pop/Rock Album

2010 Meus Prêmios Nick Awards
Favorite International Artist

2010 MTV Brazil Music Awards
International Artist

2010 MTV Europe Music Awards
Best Male
Best Push Act

2010 MTV Video Music Awards
Best New Artist

2010 Much Music Video Awards
UR FAVE: New Artist
UR FAVE: Canadian Video

2010 Myx Music Awards
Favorite International Video

2010 Teen Choice Awards
Choice Music: Male Artist
Choice Music: Breakout Artist Male
Choice Summer Music Star: Male
Choice Music: Pop Album

2010 TRL Awards
Best International Act

2010 Young Hollywood Awards
Newcomer of the Year

Other Achievements
King of Internet, 2010 most searched person on Google
Top 12 Most Charitable Celebrities of the Year 2010
No. 1 most viewed video ('Baby') in 2010

justin wordsearch

E T S G R P U F F B Y R G R E
Q V W K T R G A A T E J E M G
B B O Q G Y V B Y B Q V I U J
W D R L C U Y B E X E T M V Z
P L A J O S J I I N E I P T M
G O V P Y T B W Y N B D K S A
L K C C U N Y A O S K E P C N
Y G M Q I E S D H O G F E W B
C P W T V R V L O R Y L L B N
X D S R E Y O P E B J X Z Y E
C U V V L W Y S T M E Q G G U
J K E M Y W O R L D K M R L S
D N X D I T M T X B T O O V H
E I N E E M E I N E E N R S E
B I E B E R F E V E R V Z F R

BABY

BEEB

BIEBER FEVER

EENIE MEENIE

JUSTIN BIEBER

MY WORLD

NEVER SAY NEVER

ONE TIME

SOMEBODY TO LOVE

USHER

justin crossword

The crossword grid (handwritten answers):

1 Across: purple
2 Down: pisces
3 Across: abc's
4 Down: my world
5 Across: youtubes
6 Down: canada
7 Down: trumpet
8 Across: lonelygirl
9 Across: drew
9 Down: pa...
10 Across: french

Across

1 What is Justin's favourite colour?

3 Who beat JT to sign up Justin?

5 On what website did Justin first find
fame?

8 If you were Justin's girlfriend, you would
be One Less what?

9 What is Justin's middle name?

10 Justin is multi-talented. He speaks
English and what other language?

Down

2 What star sign is Justin?

4 What is the name of Justin's first album?

6 What country did Justin grow up in?

7 Apart from guitar, piano and drums, what
other instrument can Justin play?

BIEBER FEVER
Justin doesn't like clowns.

POP IDOL

Justin recalls the competition: 'I entered a local singing competition called Stratford Idol. The other people in the competition had been taking singing lessons and had vocal coaches. I wasn't taking it too seriously at the time, I would just sing around the house. I was only 12 and I got second place... my mum posted the video for other friends and family to see on YouTube and people seemed to really like it.'

Encouraged by the popularity of his first vid, Justin began posting more videos of him performing. His favourite covers at the time included songs by artists such as Usher, Ne-Yo and Stevie Wonder. Soon enough he started to build a lot of momentum and people all over the world were logging on to watch the latest teen sensation. Without any publicity or management, Justin notched up almost 10 million views on his YouTube account purely by word of mouth. It really was that simple, says Justin: 'I put my singing videos from the competition on YouTube so that my friends and family could watch them. But it turned out that other people liked them and they started subscribing to them.'

BIEBER FEVER
Justin says 'Smile' 36 times in the song 'U Smile'.

TRUE BELIEBER
Justin can play the drums, the trumpet, the guitar and the piano. Plus he can rap and break dance!

WE ♥ JUSTIN!

That any of the wider world would stand up and take notice of Justin was beyond his wildest dreams. 'I was just posting videos online for fun. I never thought it was possible. I never really dreamed of it.' He never imagined that anyone would click onto his YouTube account let alone the music biz's top stars.

Justin's talent was out there and the power of the Internet was propelling him to stardom at an unmanageable pace. Record execs began making enquiries into this young kid who'd gathered millions of fans just through uploading videos. It was a crazy time, recalls Justin: 'We were getting calls from lots of different managements and my mum didn't really know what was going on, or if it was real.' Within a matter of months of his mum uploading his first performance, Justin was meeting with A-list stars keen to get his signature.

SO SO DEF

Through former So So Def marketing executive Scooter Braun – who flew the then 13-year-old singer to Atlanta – Justin was introduced to Usher. Well, he actually introduced himself! 'Right when we flew into Atlanta, Scooter drove us to the studio and Usher was there in the parking lot,' remembers Justin. 'That was my first time ever being out of Canada so I went up to him and was like, 'Hey Usher, I love your songs, do you want me to sing you one?' He was like, 'No little buddy, just come inside, it's cold out.'

Justin was being introduced to a world that was totally unbelievable just a couple of months beforehand. His trip to Atlanta was a big deal in many ways. It was the first time he had ever been on a plane. And he got to meet a major pop star! 'First time I was ever on an airplane,' says Justin. 'It was amazing. I met Jermaine [Dupri, founder of So So Def], and then about a week later my manager had showed Usher the videos of me online.' Can you imagine?

Usher: factfile

Like Justin, Usher found fame at a young age. Spotted by R&B mogul L.A Reid at the tender age of 13 at a 'Star Search' competition, Usher released his first single 'Call Me a Mack' when he was just 15! As Usher says, 'I had been building my career since I was a boy ... it was all about the music'. With an instant record deal, he went on to release countless Billboard chart toppers and smash hit albums – today he has sold over 65 million records, making him one of the biggest artists of all time! With classic R&B tracks as 'Pop Ya Collar', 'Love in this Club' it's no surprise that the all-dancing, all-singing mogul saw potential in Justin! Not only is his album *Confessions* ranked as the top solo album of the last decade, but he is also considered by his fans to be the sexiest man alive. And as if glittering music career isn't enough for the gorgeous, multi-talented star, he has also has his own record label, appeared in Hollywood films and he has started his own charity, New Look, as well as owning a basketball team. Phew! Lets hope Justin follows in his mentor's footsteps...

BIEBER FEVER
Justin shares the same birthday with Ke$ha – 1 March.

HANGIN' WITH USHER

Having later seen his videos, Usher was quick to get Justin back for a proper meeting but soon other superstars started catching wind of the young starlet and Justin's signature was in high demand. 'Usher was like, 'That was the kid? Man, that kid is ... I should have let him sing for me.' And so, he flew me back to Atlanta where I got to sing for him and meet him. He then wanted to sign me. And then he got in contact with Justin Timberlake and JT also wanted to sign me.'

In the end JB decided to go with Usher, who was offering the better deal. 'A week later Usher flew me back to Atlanta,' says Justin. 'I sang for him and his people and he really wanted to sign me there and then but I still had a meeting with Justin Timberlake who also wanted to sign me. It turned out Usher's deal was way better. He had L.A. Reid backing him up and Scooter had a lot of really good connections in Atlanta. I always tease Usher now and remind him he how he blew me off the first time we met.'

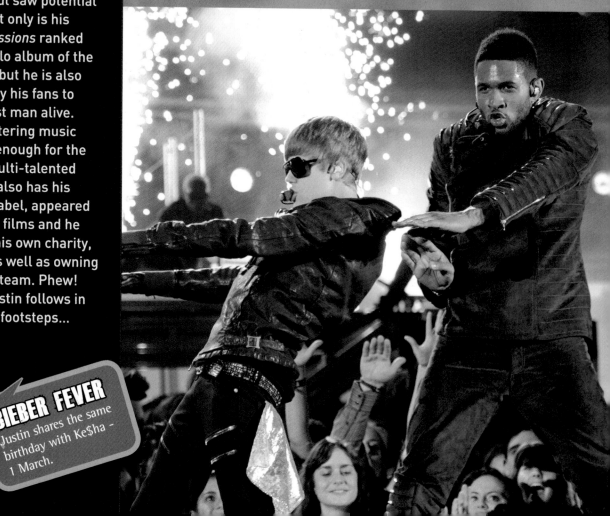

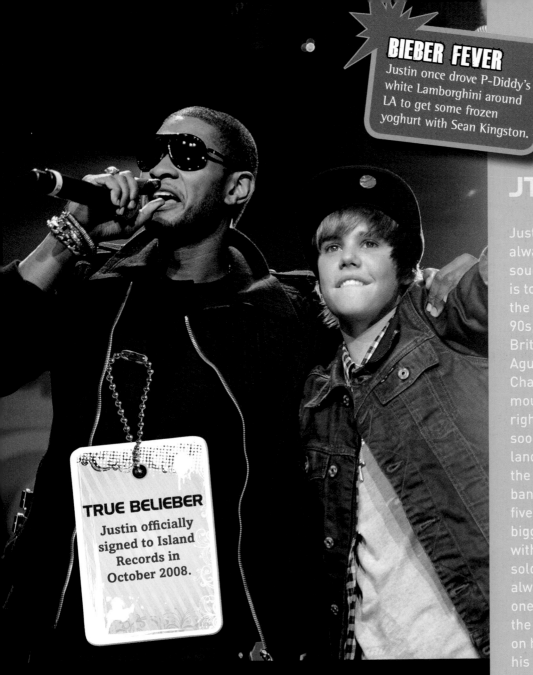

TRUE BELIEBER

Justin officially signed to Island Records in October 2008.

HANGIN' WITH JT

But while Justin was impressed with his meeting with Justin Timberlake, he was more impressed with the company. According to JB his favourite part of meeting Timberlake was meeting his then girlfriend, Jessica Biel. 'That was the best part,' says Justin. 'She is so hot'.

'I sang for him and his people and he really wanted to sign me there and then!'

JT: factfile

Justin Timberlake wasn't always the smooth-talking, soulful R&B performer he is today – he found fame on the Mickey Mouse Club in the 90s, with fellow pop stars Britney Spears, Christina Aguilera and bandmate, JC Chasez. But dressing up in mouse ears set Justin on the right track for his career – soon after leaving Disney he landed his first job, as one of the members of heartthrob band *NSync! The gorgeous fivesome became on of the biggest boybands in history, with over 65 millions records sold worldwide. But it was always clear that there was one bandmember who had the X Factor – Justin! Braving on his own, Justin released his first album, *Justified*, and never looked back. With his Michael Jackson-inspired dance moves and catchy hits such as 'Like I Love You', 'Cry Me a River' and 'Rock Your Body', Justinmania took over the world. 10 years later, Justin shows no signs of slowing down. With collaborations with the likes of Madonna, Nelly Furtado and Timbaland and an award-winning performance in the Hollywood film *The Social Network* and a clothing line, Bieber's namesake is set for one thing – world domination!

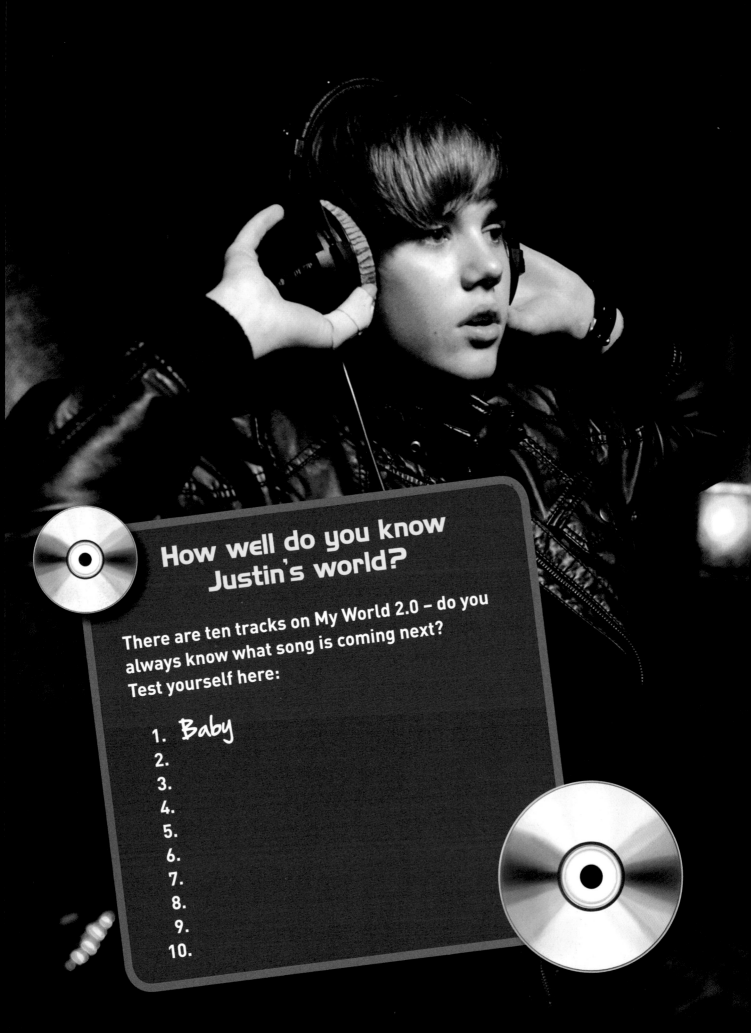

How well do you know Justin's world?

There are ten tracks on My World 2.0 – do you always know what song is coming next? Test yourself here:

1. Baby
2.
3.
4.
5.
6.
7.
8.
9.
10.

STUDIO TIME!

Even when he'd signed with a major label, JB knew that there was still a lot of work to do if he was to become a major success. Luckily Justin isn't afraid of a bit of graft and he went straight into the studio and to begin recording his first single, 'One Time'.

Justin had experience in making videos at home in front of his computer, but making the professional video for his debut single was a huge step up. They even filmed it in Usher's house! 'It was really cool going from my webcam to professional videos.'

BIEBER FEVER
While filming the 'One Less Lonely Girl' music video, the puppy in the video peed on Justin! LOL!

ONE TIME

'One Time' was Justin's first single. It was released to radio while he was still in the studio recording his debut album. The song reached number 12 in Justin's native Canada during its first week of release in July 2009 and later peaked at number 17 on the US Billboard Hot 100. The song went platinum in Canada and the U.S. and gold in the Australia and New Zealand.

BIEBER FEVER
Justin gains an average of 207,788 fans on Facebook a week.

be the next justin bieber

LEARN AN INSTRUMENT (OR TWO)...

Depending on what your talents are, it always helps to learn an instrument if you want to make it in the music biz. Remember, Justin can play loads of different things so the more the better. It doesn't matter what you play, just give it a go! And remember, practise makes perfect!

GET WRITING...

Playing cover songs is great way of getting your career up and running, but if you're serious, you should start doing your own stuff. Justin has been writing his own music for years. You could start trying to set a poem to music.

NETWORK...

Get your music to as many people as possible. Give your recordings to friends, relatives, even teachers! You never know who might end up listening to it. Another great way of getting your music out there is to set up a Myspace, YouTube, Twitter or Facebook account dedicated to your music.

PLAY LIVE...

Justin started out by busking and entering local competitions. You should do the same. Play anywhere you can in front of people. Schools and community centres are good places to start, or even just in your living room for your family. All the practice helps!

TRUE BELIEBER

Justin thinks the Internet is a major reason for his success 'It's crazy... without the Internet I would never be in this place... my fans and I have that special connection because whenever we talk on Twitter and Facebook we really have that one-on-one connection.'

MY WORLD

Justin's style was set from the off, as he sung about love and relationships in most of his debut album. He's a really sensitive soul and likes to get to the heart of the emotion behind the music. 'I love singing about love,' says Justin. 'That's what a lot of girls like listening to, and that's what I like to write. This was clearly evident in the first half of Justin's two-part debut album, *My World*, which was released on November 17, 2009 and included the three hit singles 'One Less Lonely Girl', 'Love Me', and 'Favourite Girl'. Awwww.

BIEBER FEVER
Justin doesn't like cats. He once had a dream that a cat ate him.

Justin likes to bring people into his life through his music and that was the intention with *My World*. 'It's a lot about love and teen love and what would be in my world.' But it's not just a soppy love-fest insists Justin: 'There's songs that teens can relate to, as far as parents not being together and divorced. And just stuff that happens in everyday life... real life isn't perfect, so my album kind of portrays that. You just have to make the best of what you have.' Justin writes about real life – the things that you and I experience every day. That's why his album is so powerful.

'Real life isn't perfect, so my album kind of portrays that.'

TRUE BELIEBER

Justin once kissed a poster of himself and said, 'Yup, I'm a great kisser'.

BIEBER FEVER

Justin brushes his teeth in the shower.

Ludacris: factfile

Who is Christopher Bridges? Only the 'Baby' rapper, Ludacris! Hailing from Atlanta, Georgia, Ludacris has been on the music scene since 2000 (Justin would have been 6, aww!). The fast-talking rapper started his career as a radio DJ, but it wasn't long before he got to the know the A-list and collaborated with stars such as Snoop Dogg, Pharell Williams, Sum 41, Jay-Z, Mary J Blige, and of course, Justin! And like Justin, Ludacris is good friends with Usher – the two music moguls won a Grammy award for their song 'Yeah!' in 2004. Ludacris has also turned his hand to acting – not content with writing the soundtrack for *Fast and Furious*, Ludacris starred in the series as the character, Tej! He has also been the star of films *RocknRolla*, *Max Payne* and *Repo Man*, as well having his very own Simpson's character created for him! Talk about multi-talented!

TRUE BELIEBER

Justin gets about 60 new mentions on Twitter per second whether he tweets or not.

MY WORLD 2.0

It wasn't long before *My World 2.0*, was released with catchy single 'Baby' as the lead single. The track contained Justin's first major collaboration with rap star Ludacris (or 'Luda' as Justin calls him) making an appearance. The single became Justin's biggest hit to date, charting at number five in the U.S. and reaching the top ten in seven other countries. The album was an even bigger success, though. *My World 2.0* debuted at number one on the US, Canadian, Irish, Australian and New Zealand album charts and reached the top ten in fifteen other countries. Justin was the youngest solo male act to top the US chart since Stevie Wonder in 1963.

Justin went on to release 'Somebody to Love', 'U Smile' and 'Pray' from his first two albums. He later collaborated with Willow Smith's brother, Jaden Smith, to make the track 'Never Say Never' for the film *The Karate Kid*.

TRUE BELIEBER

Just like his co-singer, Jaden Smith, in 'Never Say Never', Justin used to take karate classes when he was younger.

BIEBER FEVER

Justin says he has never drunk alcohol and doesn't want to try it.

FAME CALLS

It's very hard to believe that in just over twelve months Justin morphed from being just a regular kid playing music on his laptop to being the most famous teen on the planet. Justin can't go anywhere without being mobbed. 'It's pretty hard to comprehend. Everything is surreal' says Justin of his newfound fame. 'All my fans are really supportive, like on Twitter and everything. I'm just really glad that I get to do what I love.'

Justin's really lucky to be surrounded by solid trustworthy people, as there can be plenty of nasty folk in the record biz who would take advantage of a young star like Justin. Thankfully he has his mum with him most of the time and a select group of people who he really trusts. 'We're really sceptical on who we let into our team,' says Justin. 'We have a really small team. We have fun. We've grown to be like a family. It's been incredible.'

But despite all the hype and fame, Justin still keeps it real and doesn't let any of it go to his head. 'I still feel regular,' he says. 'You know, sometimes it's weird that I go places and I have thousands of people waiting for me, but I always think, 'I'm Justin''.

TRUE BELIEBER

What's the highlight of Justin's career so far? 'I got to perform for President Obama,' says Justin. 'That's probably at the top of things that I've done.'

BIEBER FEVER

Jazzy, Justin's little sister calls him 'Boo Boo' when she needs something.

JUST A REGULAR KID?

There aren't many peeps Justin's age who have to work as hard as he does. He can sometimes put in 18-hour days which is why he tries to take out time when he can to just goof around. 'We try and take out one day a week where I can go and be a regular kid. Just play basketball and go and hang out with my friends. Just do what I like to do. You know, some times for that day I just like to sleep, because the six days before that I've been exhausted.'

JUSTIN GETS THE FEAR

And Justin has fears and phobias like the rest of us, too. Being stuck in confined spaces. He got stuck in an elevator when he was younger. And when he was seven, he once played hide and seek with his cousin. His cousin shut him in a toy box and he got stuck in there. He's has been afraid of the dark and small spaces ever since. No wonder!

BIEBER FEVER
Even though Justin's eyes are light brown/hazel, they turn greenish in the sunlight.

TRUE BELIEBER
Justin says his favourite underwear is D&G!

date justin

So you want to go on a date with Justin? How many of his strict criteria do you meet? Tick them off and see if you're a perfect match! ✔

JUSTIN'S IDEAL GIRL...

☐ Is more about personality than looks. 'Be a nice person and someone I can talk to. Because at the end of the day you can have the hottest girl in the world but if you can't sit there and have a conversation with her it's going to be terrible.'

☐ Is naturally beautiful and doesn't wear too much make-up. 'I don't like girls who wear lots of make-up and you can't see their face,' says Justin. 'Some girls are beautiful but insecure and look much better without the make-up, but decide to put loads on.'

☐ Has pretty eyes and smile (remember to floss those teeth!). 'I like a girl with a nice smile and eyes.'

☐ Is relaxed and doesn't mind embarrassing moments. Justin can be a bit clumsy on dates. He was once with a girl at an Italian restaurant and he was wearing a white shirt. He ordered spaghetti and spilt it down the front of his shirt. Oops!

☐ Is a family person. Justin's mum is super-protective. She even tried to stop him dating until he was 16. '

☐ **Has old-fashioned values.** Justin's a traditional romantic at heart. 'I think that being a gentleman is what matters; taking them out to a nice dinner, open the doors, stuff like that. Flowers are great, but love is better – you know what I mean?'

☐ **Is a Belieber!** Justin hasn't ruled out dating fans, saying: 'It depends what the situation is. I think that I'm not going to limit myself.'

☐ **Cracks jokes!** 'I like girls that are funny because I like to laugh and joke around,' says Justin.

☐ **Has an accent.** Justin likes the sound of a foreign voice. His favourite accents are French, English and Australian. But then everyone has an accent of some sort so there's still hope!

BIEBER FEVER

Earlier this year, Twitter reported that 83% of twitter users are Justin Bieber fans. Can you imagine?

make your own justin badge

Show off to your friends that you love Justin the most with your very own homemade Justin Bieber badges.

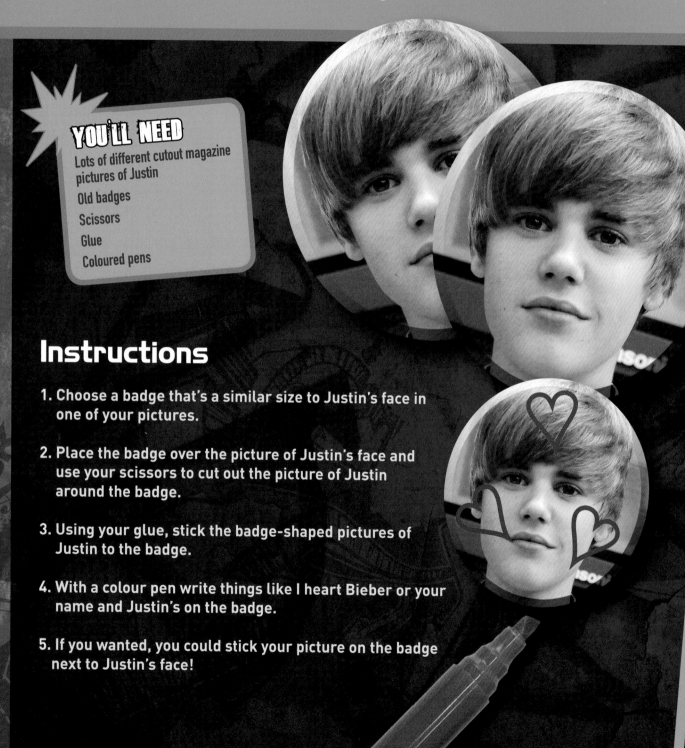

YOU'LL NEED

Lots of different cutout magazine pictures of Justin

Old badges

Scissors

Glue

Coloured pens

Instructions

1. Choose a badge that's a similar size to Justin's face in one of your pictures.

2. Place the badge over the picture of Justin's face and use your scissors to cut out the picture of Justin around the badge.

3. Using your glue, stick the badge-shaped pictures of Justin to the badge.

4. With a colour pen write things like I heart Bieber or your name and Justin's on the badge.

5. If you wanted, you could stick your picture on the badge next to Justin's face!

QUARTERS ONLY

50¢

TO OPERATE
TURN
HANDLE
ONE
FULL
TURN

2296

50¢

JUSTIN ON LOVE

TRUE BELIEBER

Justin has once tripped over his own hockey stick, while trying to impress a girl while playing hockey.

What does Justin really know about love and girls? Well not much, really. He's the first to admit that he's still young and has a lot to learn.

'I think love is like a learning process throughout your life. You learn how to be better at it and you learn more about it. I'm still learning. I'm not saying I know everything about love. I'm still trying to figure out girls... I don't think we'll ever totally figure out girls.'

BIEBER FEVER

Justin says he wants three kids. Awww!

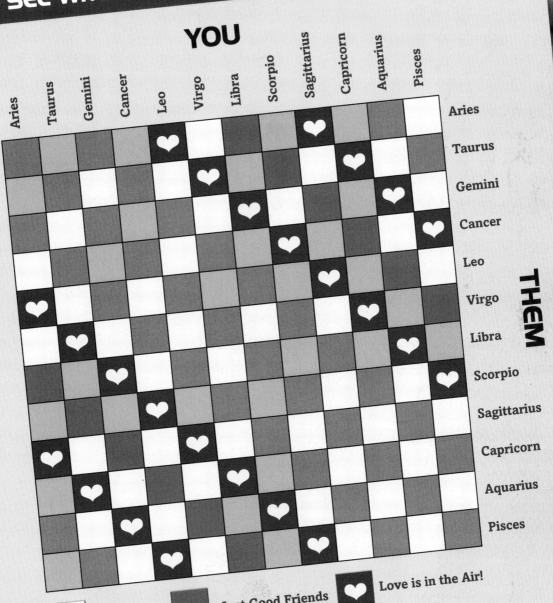

TRUE BELIEBER
Justin has called Kim Kardashian his girlfriend before but he insists he was only kidding around and they're just friends.

WHAT STAR SIGN ARE YOU? LOOK AT THIS CHART AND SEE WHO YOU ARE MOST COMPATIBLE WITH!

YOU

Aries · Taurus · Gemini · Cancer · Leo · Virgo · Libra · Scorpio · Sagittarius · Capricorn · Aquarius · Pisces

THEM

Aries · Taurus · Gemini · Cancer · Leo · Virgo · Libra · Scorpio · Sagittarius · Capricorn · Aquarius · Pisces

No Way!

Awkward!

Just Good Friends

There's Potential

 Love is in the Air!

JUSTIN & SELENA - IS IT ON?

OMG! Could it be that potentially the cutest two people in showbiz are getting together? With strong rumours for and against the relationship, and JB keeping quiet, who knows? There has been lots of talk about the couple hanging out together and even going on the odd date, but for the moment, Justin has been pretty shy about the whole relationship stating: 'She's one of my best friends. Some things you just gotta keep to yourself.'

And when it comes to Valentine's it sounds like Justin only has eyes for one person... his mum! 'I have one person that I'll be sending flowers to and that's my mum. She's been there since the beginning and has given up a lot for me, I'm very blessed to have her. She likes roses.'

TRUE BELIEBER

Justin is allowed to pick the girls for his videos. 'Yeah, they let me pick,' says Justin. Lucky guy!

TRUE BELIEBER

Justin had his first kiss aged 13, at a school dance. He made the first move (song playing: How to 'Save A Life' by the Fray).

love is in the air

So, you want to make Justin's heart flutter this Valentine's Day? Create the most romantic card to make him weak at the knees.

Instructions

1. Fold one of the pieces of paper in half.

2. From the folded side, cut out a half-heart shape about 7cm into the paper. You should now have a symmetrical heart.

3. Fold the picture or magazine cut-out in half, and cut a half-heart shape from the folded side.

4. Stick the heart-shaped picture of Justin to the heart-shaped card or paper.

5. Fold the second piece of card or paper in half. Glue the outside of the heart card to the second card.

6. Now fold the edge of the glitter paper in by 2cm and cut six half-heart shapes out of the vertically folded strip. Do this four or five times until you have around 25 or so hearts.

7. Put the glitter hearts inside the card, so when he opens the card hearts will sprinkle onto his lap.

IF YOU LIKE, YOU CAN WRITE A POEM INSIDE...

Roses are red,
Violets are blue,
But most of all, Justin,
I love you x

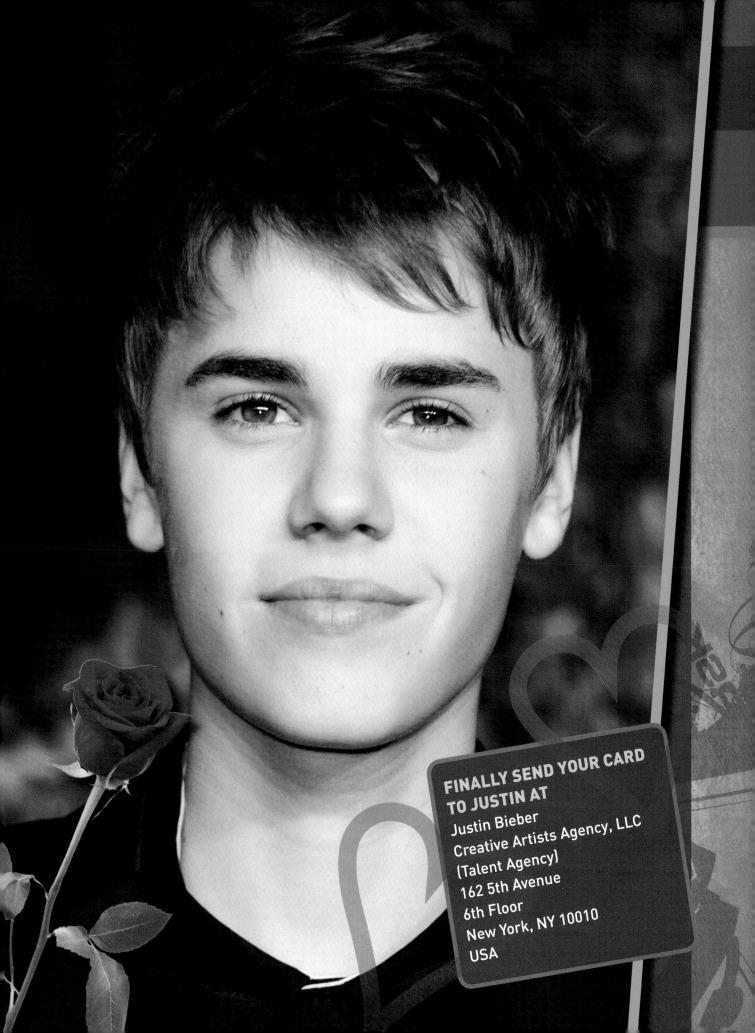

FINALLY SEND YOUR CARD TO JUSTIN AT

Justin Bieber
Creative Artists Agency, LLC
(Talent Agency)
162 5th Avenue
6th Floor
New York, NY 10010
USA

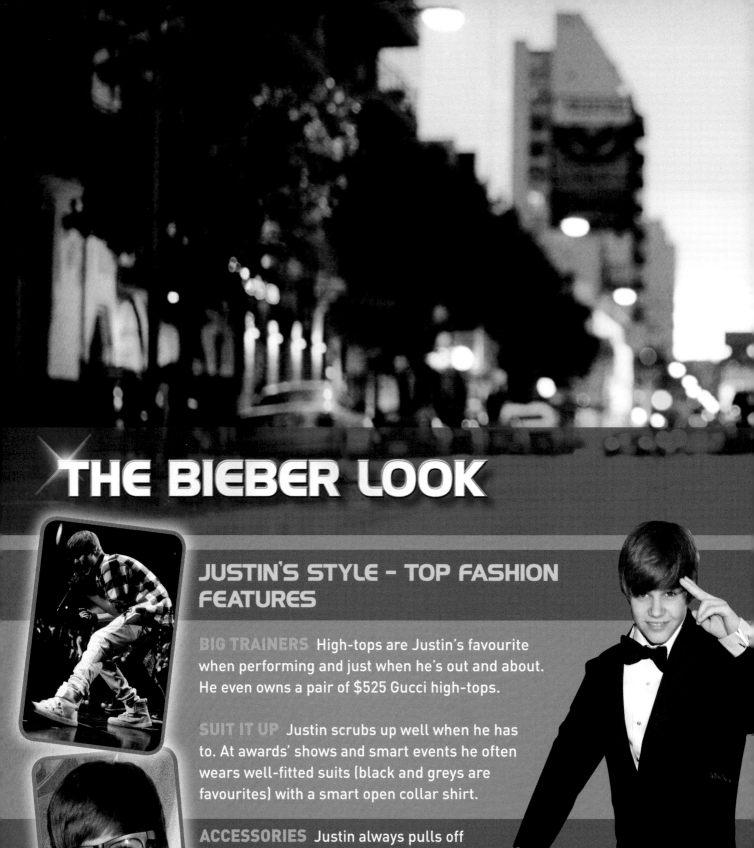

THE BIEBER LOOK

JUSTIN'S STYLE – TOP FASHION FEATURES

BIG TRAINERS High-tops are Justin's favourite when performing and just when he's out and about. He even owns a pair of $525 Gucci high-tops.

SUIT IT UP Justin scrubs up well when he has to. At awards' shows and smart events he often wears well-fitted suits (black and greys are favourites) with a smart open collar shirt.

ACCESSORIES Justin always pulls off wearing glasses. He definitely rocks them so they're more chic than geek!

PLAIN AND BOLD When dressing casual, Justin will always set off plain colours against a bold accessory. A classic look is dark jeans and shirt with a bright coloured scarf and trainers. Classic Justin!

THE SMART-CASH JACKET Justin will often go for the rolled-up sleeve jacket or the slightly smarter sports or suit jacket over a pair of jeans – good for almost any occasion.

THE GRUNGE LOOK He maybe a pop star but Justin fits in with any rocker when he wears his one of his gingham shirts (usually purple or black) with a black t-shirt underneath.

WHERE'S YOUR HAIR AT?

JB gave us all a shock when he walked out onto the Golden Globe Awards with an all-new hair cut! He's famous for his brushed forward moptop haircut, but Justin thinned his fringe and has gone for a more messy and textured look on the top, rather than his usual flop across fringe. Apparently 80,000 followers stopped following him on Twitter after the snip. Thankfully, to the rest of the 8 million of us still following him, he still looks hot!

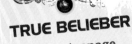

TRUE BELIEBER

Some teenage boys are paying £100 to get Justin's hairstyle! Can you imagine?

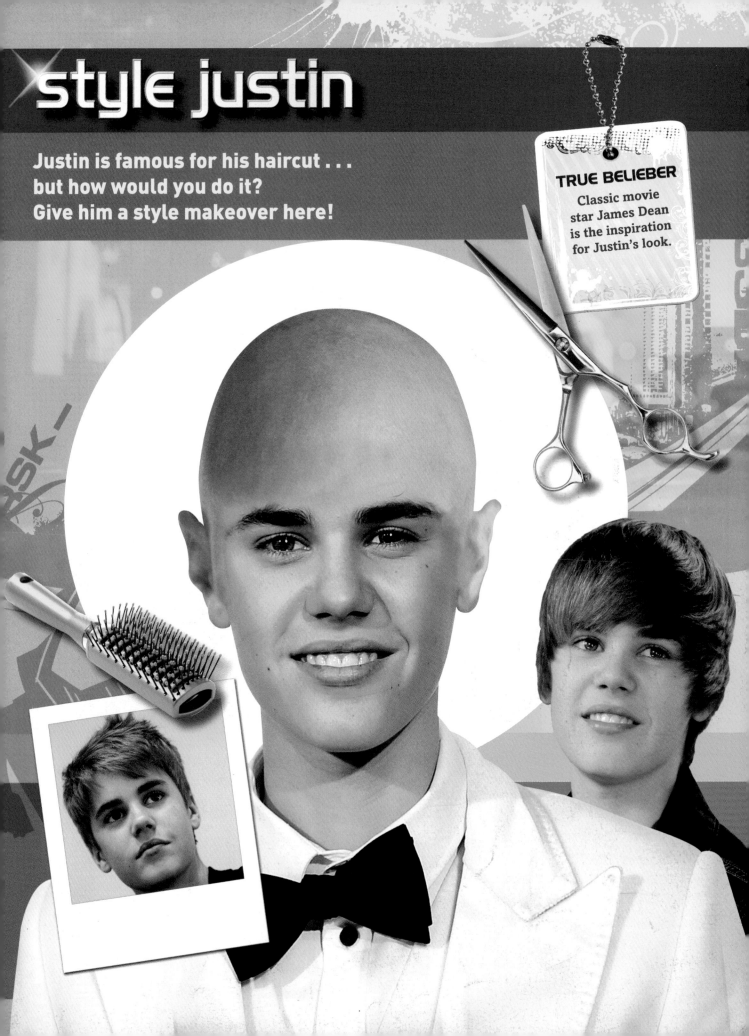

style justin

Justin is famous for his haircut . . .
but how would you do it?
Give him a style makeover here!

TRUE BELIEBER
Classic movie star James Dean is the inspiration for Justin's look.

justin's birthday quiz

Do you know enough about Justin to spend time with him on his birthday? Take the Justin birthday challenge to find out...

1. First you'll need to know when the special day is, when is Justin's birthday?
A) March 1st
B) May 1st
C) April 1st
D) Feb 22nd

2. For Justin's birthday breakfast treat what would he like to eat?
A) Cornflakes
B) Eggs
C) Coco Pops
D) Captain Crunch

3. Justin often likes to play sport on his days off, but on his birthday what would his favourite game to play be?
A) Ice hockey
B) Baseball
C) Football
D) Basketball

4. You make Justin a birthday cake. What common cake ingredient DOESN'T he like?
A) Icing
B) Banana
C) Chocolate
D) Strawberry

5. Justin wants a guitar for his birthday, what is different about Justin's guitars?
A) They're all acoustic
B) They're all electric
C) They're left-handed
D) They're right-handed

6. What kind of present would Justin be LEAST impressed with?
A) Car
B) Laptop
C) Trainers
D) Jewellry

7. If Justin could go to the pictures and watch any movie what would it be?
A) *Rocky*
B) *High School Musical*
C) *Hannah Montana*
D) *Pirates of the Caribbean*

8. You go out for Justin's birthday date. What time is his curfew?
A) 9.30pm
B) 10pm
C) 11pm
D) 11.30pm

9. What does Justin like most in a girl?
A) Good looks
B) Confidence
C) Intelligence
D) Personality

10. To get to Justin, you first have to impress his mum. What are her favourite flowers?
A) Roses
B) Tulips
C) Carnations
D) Sunflowers

See p 61 for the answers!

HOW DID YOU SCORE? DID YOU GET ENOUGH POINTS TO HANG OUT WITH JUSTIN ON HIS BIG DAY?

0-2 – You need to learn more about Justin if you're going to make him feel special on his birthday.

3-5 – Not bad, Justin might make time for a quick coffee with you on his special day.

6-8 – You sure know your stuff; you get an invite to Justin's birthday party

9+ – Lucky you! You get to spend the whole day with Justin.

WHAT'S UP NEXT?

JUSTIN IN 3D!

Justin recently released the 3D movie, *Never Say Never*, charting his rise to fame. Every true fan must see it. The flick shows Justin as you've never seen him on-screen before. Visually it's stunning, with 3D live performances. But displaying himself in full-on three dimensions was quite daunting for image-conscious Justin, who had to make sure his skin was clear of any spots before filming! 'It's not really a concert movie but it kind of shows my story' he says. 'It was kind of cool to see myself so big but at the same time I was a little... what's the word? It made me feel self-conscious because your face is so big that you can see everything.'

JUST BEING JUSTIN

With his career going nova, Justin is eager to get off the music treadmill and make sure he gets to take some time-out to be himself and get up to some non-work fun too! 'I like to do regular kids stuff' says Justin. 'I like to play golf, I like to go to the movies with my friends. I like to shoot hoops,' says Justin. Justin is also a bit of an adrenaline junky and loves skateboarding. When he was in New Zealand he went bungee jumping! Most of all he loves hockey, 'I love hockey. I played hockey all my life.'

TRUE BELIEBER

Justin always wanted to be a car mechanic when he was younger, so he was really happy with Usher's birthday present for his sweet 16. 'I got a Range Rover.'

Form your own belieber fan club

Starting a fan club is a fab way of meeting and getting to know other Beliebers out there. It's also great for sharing info, tips and gossip about Justin.

WHERE?

First you need to decide where you're going to have your club. You could have weekly meetings in your room or classroom at break-time. Alternatively you could set up a Myspace, Bebo, Twitter or Facebook page, dedicated to Justin. By going online you could meet fellow Justin fans from around the world.

WHEN?

You then have to decide how often you're going to hold meetings. You could do a weekly get-together with all your Belieber pals, or if you're super-keen you could do it daily. Saturday afternoons are always a good time as no-one has school. If you're online you could arrange time for Instant Messenger chats with all your new Bieber-mad pals.

ACTIVITIES

Now that your group is all set up, you'll need some stuff to do. All the activities in this book would be a good place to start. You can all play the Bieber quiz game and see who has the highest score. Or you can see who can make the prettiest Valentine's Day card for Justin. Or you could make videos of yourselves singing Justin Bieber's best songs to upload onto YouTube!

Club meetings or online forums are a good way of sharing and catching up on all the latest Bieber goss. You can also show off and share your latest posters.

But the best thing to do in a Justin Bieber fan club is to get all the Justin CDs, YouTube clips and movies and get everyone over to yours or a friend's house to have a Bieber-fest of music and videos.

TICK OFF THE BIEBER DISCOGRAPHY BELOW. HAVE YOU GOT ALL THE BIEBER ALBUMS, SINGLES AND REMIXES AT YOUR FAN CLUB?

ALBUMS

- ☑ My World 2.0
- ☐ My World
- ☐ My Worlds Acoustic
- ☐ Never Say Never – The Remixes
- ☐ My Worlds: The Collection

SINGLES

- ☐ 'One Time'
- ☐ 'One Less Lonely Girl'
- ☐ 'Baby'
- ☐ 'Somebody to Love'
- ☐ 'U Smile'
- ☐ 'Pray'
- ☐ 'Never Say Never'

DVD'S

- ☐ This is My World

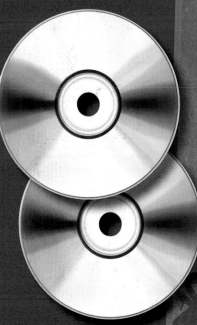

JUSTIN DISCUSSION TOPICS

At your meetings – let's call them parties! – it's really fun to start some discussions to find out what other fans think of JB too. Fill in your answers here and find out what other people in your fan club think on these hot Bieber topics.

What is Justin's best song?

Who should Justin work with in the future?

Should Justin do more acting?

What is Justin's best hairstyle?

What should Justin get his mother or girlfriend for Christmas?

What is your favourite Justin Youtube clip?

Should there be a *My World 3.0*?

Who should JB date?

Will Justin win an Oscar or a Grammy in the future?

answers

Quiz - pages 10-11

1. C) Drew
2. D) 1994
3. D) Pisces
4. B) Kidrauhl
5. A) Sammy
6. B) J – Bone
7. A) Smallville
8. C) Chuck Norris
9. D) 13
10. D) James Dean
11. A) Ludakris
12. C) Canadian
13. C) Justin Timberlake
14. B) Saxophone
15. A) A holiday
16. D) A car
17. A) Atlanta
18. D) Jazmine and Jackson
19. B) Purple
20. C) Ryan Butler

Quiz - page 52

1. A) March 1st
2. D) Captain Crunch
3. D) Basketball
4. C) Chocolate
5. C) They're left-handed
6. D) Jewellry
7. A) Rocky
8. B) 10pm
9. D) Personality
10. A) Roses

Wordsearch - page 20

E	T	S	G	R	P	U	F	F	B	Y	R	G	R	E
Q	V	W	K	T	R	G	A	A	T	E	J	E	M	G
B	B	O	Q	G	Y	V	B	Y	B	Q	V	I	U	J
W	D	R	L	C	U	Y	B	E	X	E	T	M	V	Z
P	L	A	J	O	S	J	I	I	N	E	I	P	T	M
G	O	V	P	Y	T	B	W	Y	N	D	K	S	A	M
L	K	C	C	U	N	Y	A	O	S	K	E	P	C	N
Y	G	M	Q	I	E	S	D	H	O	G	F	E	W	B
C	P	W	T	X	R	V	L	O	R	Y	L	L	B	N
X	D	S	R	E	Y	O	P	E	B	J	X	Z	Y	E
C	U	V	L	W	Y	S	T	M	E	Q	G	Q	U
J	K	E	M	Y	W	O	R	L	D	K	M	R	L	S
D	N	X	D	I	T	M	T	X	B	T	O	O	V	H
E	I	N	E	E	M	E	I	N	E	E	N	R	S	E
B	I	E	B	E	R	F	E	V	E	R	V	Z	F	R

Crossword - page 21

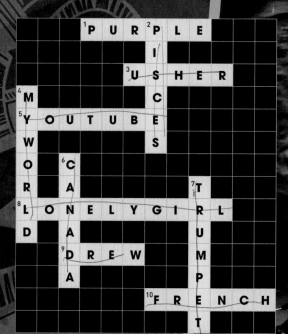

1. PURPLE
2. PI(CS)
3. USHER
4. M
5. YOUTUBE
6. CA
7. T
8. LONELYGIRL
9. DREW
10. FRENCH

BIEBER FEVER

It takes less than 30 seconds for one of Justin's tweets to be re-tweeted 100 times.

First published in hardback in Great Britain in 2011 by
Orion Books an imprint of the Orion Publishing Group Ltd
Orion House, 5 Upper St Martin's Lane, London WC2H 9EA
An Hachette UK Company

10 9 8 7 6 5 4 3 2 1

A CIP catalogue record for this book is available from the British Library.

ISBN: 978 14091 4124 2

Designed by carrstudio.co.uk
Printed in Italy by Rotolito

The Orion Publishing Group's policy is to use papers that are natural,
renewable and recyclable and made from wood grown in sustainable forests.
The logging and manufacturing processes are expected to conform to the
environmental regulations of the country of origin.

Every effort has been made to fulfil requirements with regard to reproducing
copyright material. The author and publisher will be glad to rectify any
omissions at the earliest opportunity.

www.orionbooks.co.uk

PICTURE CREDITS
All pictures courtesy of Getty Images.
All background images courtesy of
istockphoto.

ACKNOWLEDGEMENTS
Posy Edwards would like to Guyan
Mitra, Jane Sturrock, Nicola Crossley,
Helen Ewing and Rich Carr.